Son of a Cult:

A Longitudinal Study

Son of a Cult:

A Longitudinal Study

Poems by

Allen C. Jones

Cover design by Shay Culligan
Cover image: *Bust of Akehenaten* (1908), Smith, Joseph
Lindon (1863–1950). Isabella Stewart Gardner Museum,
Boston, MA, USA© Isabella Stewart Gardner Museum
/Bridgeman Images.

ISBN: 978-1-63980-343-9

Kelsay Books
502 South 1040 East, A-119
American Fork, Utah 84003
Kelsaybooks.com

Other Books by the Author

Her Death was Also Water

For my fellow "Groupers,"

who each have their own stories

of that time.

Contents

"Once the dream of paradise starts to turn into reality . . .
people begin to crop up who stand in its way,
and so the rulers of paradise must build a little gulag
on the side of Eden."

—Milan Kundera

Killing Akhenaten

After Joseph Lindon Smith's *The Bust of Akhenaten*

Dear god-child,
you who sought to monopolize
divinity,
when your advisors attacked you,
I wonder if you used
the god-eye,
that trick they teach pharaohs,
a real killer in meetings
but futile
against the knife.
And how did your subjects feel
embalming
your slender body,
fitting the crown
to your shattered skull,
brutally cocooning your corpse
in its godhood?
Isn't this the definition
of loyalty?
I found you framed in Boston,
offering up
your perfect neck,
as if ready for the blade.
Crimson paint
spattered your ear,
and I wondered what artist
would mar
his ghostly masterpiece.
Then I thought of my own gods,
in this case
the woman who raised me
in her cult,

how hundreds chose her
then dethroned her.
I thought
of the pharaoh's gaze she cast
across a room,
the dread and hope
that she would choose me,
a boy forever
dreaming of a pedestal,
and how she might
now watch
my hand tremble
as I force myself to write this,
each word a drop
pulsing across the page.

Childhood

A Leader Needs a Legend

She was born in the final days
of the British Raj.
It is said,
Brahmins proffered themselves
before her pram begging
her nanny
to roll over them.
Oh yes.
She met the great mystics,
a child prodigy
who sat in a circle of students
and read minds,
quick as a magician flipping cards
—King of hearts,
Jack of clubs—
the right one every time.
Imagine
the side effects
of such a superpower.
She married an actor in New York
birthed five children
then escaped his philandering
in a VW bus
west to California,
reading every mind she met,
the highway a cacophony
of lust, loss, and jeremiad,
her golden locks flying
out the window,
for she was stunning.
Oh yes.
She bought a sacred mountain
for she was also rich.

What we Americans call
a double whammy.
Her husband begged forgiveness
then stole
her secret knowledge
in late night conversation.
Armed with esoteric
pillow talk,
it was he who started the cult.
Oh yes.
And it was the kind of cult
you're thinking of.
A fine actor,
he played both
King of hearts and Jack of clubs
(sex and violence
his lesson
from those post-coital chats).
Apparently, love
blinds even the great mystics,
so it took years before
she saw
the man behind the curtain.
She had to storm
her own husband's compound.
When men drew guns
at the gates,
her mythical golden hair
proved
quite bulletproof.
It is said
she simply led the women away,
offering to teach them.

A single rule: no fucking around.
The men followed,
as men do.
And so my people came to be,
spawning
to five hundred,
and no one fucked around,
a feat
more miraculous than parting
a seawater inlet.
But there were other rules.
Oh yes.
And five hundred minds
she could not silence,
lusting, losing, and perpetually editing
jeremiads.
She liked to compare herself to Moses,
we her people,
though she made it clear
we were more lost than chosen.
I ponder those tablets.
Were there ten,
or did the old prophet shuffle them
like a magician?
Did his people check the handwriting?
We certainly didn't.

First Lesson

My parents catch
Miranda and I
noticing our figures
in a bath at age four.
In a cold kitchen
they lecture us
on the unsexed shape
of the human heart.
I recall my soles
sticking to linoleum,
the scent of apple soap,
and two naked children
who will forget for years.
These days, angel gangs
roam Eden, legacies lost,
and Miranda is married,
but if I'm passing through,
I climb the gate, sneak
back into the compound,
and rest an hour in that tub.

A Tiny Solar System Called the Heart

In 1979, as Pluto slips inside Neptune's orbit,
I bring The Leader flowers the first day of school.
Miranda is jealous. This registers on no instrument.

On the way to school, as the Sony Walkman
hits the shelves, I stare at the sun,
sure I am superhuman. Miranda laughs.

As Three Mile Island melts, Miranda runs
ahead and tells The Leader about the flowers.
So sweet, she says, as I pull Miranda's hair.

The Leader asks me why I'm so angry.
I want to explain the vertigo of hope,
how the tiniest betrayal can topple us.

But I'm only five, and already I know
boys don't cry and flowers are no more
important than my troubling dreams.

Decades later I see Miranda at a funeral.
The world has grown crueler, so it's easy
to talk of war rather than what we've lost.

As we part, I offer Miranda the flowers
I've kept all these years for The Leader.
She shakes my hand as if closing a deal.

Pluto returns, restoring order to the heavens.
It won't stray again until long after we die.
But the sun remains dangerously bright.

Why I Am a Writer

Weirdoes did strange things
in our barn
until the cops came
and trundled them away.
My parents bolted the doors,
so naturally,
we kids broke in.
The weirdoes had bequeathed us
a hoard
of memorabilia and machine parts
arranged carefully
as a puzzle.
We spent months
mulling over their logic.
What binds motors,
the 1970s,
and cans of inflammables?
Testing hypotheses,
we burned down the barn,
nearly the town.
Our parents said, *What the hell!*
The barn is ash,
but I still spend my nights there.
You might think
I'm a weirdo,
sorting these charred bits,
walking around
with blackened fingertips,
but I'm building
a machine
to ignite the past,
shoveling every legible detail
into the boiler.

I feed it anything I can,
pausing only
to listen for parents
or sirens.

Children of Utopia

Autumn in the prison of youth means Top Ramen afternoons between cartoons and a warped pool table, strutting slit-eyed like Technicolor tough guys with gangster accents, hunting for designer labels on our hand -me-downs, aroused by the power of rhyme when my brother says *Slob my nob* and chalks his cue. When winter comes like a broken promise, howling through the breezeway, shifting every shot, destroying the truth of angles, and the money for ramen runs out, and even the animated world of opulent ducks cannot pacify us, we shove our acned bodies into the yard, pulverize concrete blocks with sledge hammers, pin each other down in the mud to convey the joy of youth, and think little of unbreakable bodies. Then, because this is California, the sun comes out, someone buys us noodles, every shot is a slow-motion miracle, the pool table gulping the balls like water, and the voice on the television assures us, you will get the girl, you will find the gold, and ramen will fall from the sky.

I Will Make You Fishermen

Home from war,
she-devils inked on his chest,

uncle Abe recruits us
to swear and fish.

We cut bamboo poles,
and troop to the creek

to hunt shadows.
He tells us to walk soft

as soldiers. Fish sonar
can sense each step.

I stamp in disbelief.
A trout leaps,

sun platinum on its back.
Not one bite shivers

our hand-wound lines,
punishment for clumsy feet,

then on my hook,
too weak to pull,

a thumb-sized fry dangles,
and because it dies,

I carry it home,
cupped like a pet in my palm.

My uncle crisps it
in butter, so small

I can eat the bones.
Toss the damn head,

he says, but I slip
the dime-sized skull

into a napkin, awed
by the size of my hands.

Outside I play at war,
spoils in my pocket,

believing my step alone
summoned that silver fish.

I Learn About the Mean Streets

Strictest of the parents,
my father forbids rock music,
but uncle Abe loves his eight track
and sings while driving us.
We smuggle a tape recorder
under a sweater, pirating
a mix of pop hits
and carpool chatter,
then lie in our bunk whispering
Come sail away,
one ear pressed to the deck,
one to the door.
My father catches us
but is an understanding man,
so as a lesson
we listen to Thriller together,
and he carefully cites
The Leader's thoughts
applying them to Mr. Jackson.
He is my father,
commander of the candy money
the chow,
and most of my heart,
so I hide my face from his babble
as I softly croon, *Beat it.*
He doesn't see
that I'm already eight,
high time to prepare myself
for the mean streets.
I don't recall
if my father let Mr. Jackson
into the house that day,
and he will argue for hours

with uncle Abe
about the eight track,
but the world streams toward us
on every channel,
penetrating the walls
with radio waves,
until one evening,
driving us home from school,
even uncle Abe cuts the eight track
and slams the car to a halt.
We wait for him to quote The Leader.
He just says,
Forget it,
then opens the door and leaves.
No one moves.
To chase him is to accept
the specter of desertion.
Each of us examines
what we have said and done,
suddenly afraid
we have the power to undo a man.
Only the youngest,
Miranda, dares to go after him.
And I realize
that all this time
she has carried a strength
I cannot comprehend.
She will run away with uncle,
discarding his title as normal people do.
Just as the mean streets
rise up to swallow us all,
steps sound,
uncle's weight shifts the car

back into balance,
the car fan roars heat across our faces,
and headlights open
a tunnel through the darkness.
We are hushed
except Miranda who sings,
It's so urgent,
so softly the pop song
seems a prayer.

An Emphasis on Student Engagement

When The Leader descends
on the school,
we prepare ourselves
for a five hour nonsensical lecture,
but in fifth grade
we have a public school kid.
From day one,
I have secretly examined him,
copying his walk,
rolling my pants like his,
and begging my parents
for the same white Converse.
Now I only hope
The Leader doesn't do anything crazy.
This is when
she pulls up her dress
to show us one of her breasts.
I watch the new kid
and want to say,
The Leader means well,
but there's no getting over
that boob.
No way this happens at other schools.
She said something like,
We all fed here once,
cupping herself like a club.
I was amazed
that the public school kid
just sat there
like the rest of us,
waiting to play football again.
I'm sure he never told
his parents,

though he didn't re-enroll.
If someone asked me for a metaphor,
I'd say this:
Memory is like a sailor on a sinking ship.
We jettison most of our life
to stay afloat,
then one day we come to this breast,
lounging about on deck.
It won't budge
and refuses to say a thing.

Student of the Celestial

At twelve I care only for dusk,
to lie in the square of gold
Miranda's window cuts from night,
chewing the sweet from straw,
waiting for a silhouetted breast,
bliss as mathematical as a curve.
I'm sure she knows, removing
enough shirts to clothe an army.
But as great truths are depthless,
I know it's best to fail, face the sky,
chew straw to a tasteless paste,
gaze up at the Seven Sisters,
discover to this day, only six.

Such a Little Thing

Once,
comparing tans,
Miranda turned her back,
shirt rising in her hands.
Higher, I said,
shivering with desire,
until a sliver
of white breast
dropped free.
Very tan, I mumbled.
We traded massages,
though she never
took a turn.
I never complained,
rubbing every part of her
the law allowed.
Once,
she rolled over
in the heavy heat
of afternoon
and lay beneath me,
eyes closed,
not an inch of back
in sight.
My entire body
was a tremor stopped in time.
For years I cursed myself,
but now
I love that shy boy.
Once,
before her family
went away,
we both looked nowhere,

as I gently slipped
my hand between her legs.
Such a little thing
to do,
but we held our breath
like freedivers.
Just then,
her father burst in,
hands trembling,
ready to murder me.
Hello uncle,
I said,
dizzy with fear,
holding up his title
like a shield.

First Loss

for Charlotte

You laughed at me. I wished
dark things on you as a lesson.
I was twelve, you were eleven.
That year they found the cells,

terrible in their darkness. The lesson
was once removed: my memory
of your last year is its own cell. I find
myself there, still unsaying my words.

Once you pulled off your headscarf
after your hair was gone. Dark lakes
made a relief map across your skin.
Your scarf lay still, heavy as wet hair.

The quiet in that room asked for words,
Need anything? I asked. You laughed,
said, *Not another scarf,* and turned
to face the last year of your life.

Stolen Child

There's a story of a child
stolen from his clan.
He grows to love his new family.
They call him brother.
I forget the rest.
In real life,
I see him years later,
and insist
he reminisce.
His wife is perturbed,
wondering why
I'm so enthusiastic,
when my family stole
her husband.
We'll always be brothers,
I say, clinking
his glass,
forever on page one.

Poems on the Battlefield

The stars may rule our fate,
but reading them is never easy,

the open hand of one man's
constellation, another man's knife.

The Taira samurai armor
comes to our local museum.

Butterflies mark their banners,
symbols of beauty and transformation.

The creatures look violent,
sprouting wings a brutal occupation.

We learn of the poet Yorimasa,
a Taira friend who turned on them.

Defeated, he wrote a poem
then invented ritual suicide.

Only a poet could think
such a transformation beautiful.

That day, I overhear that Jonah
will come live with my family.

I picture us samurai warriors,
writing poems during battles.

Thinking this beautiful, I tell him:
The Leader will make us brothers.

His face falls like a creature
shorn of its wings.

I hate you, he says,
eying me like an enemy.

I try to write this poem
until the day grows dark.

When the stars come out,
I cannot name a single one.

The First Crack

the uncle   I will not name

                      is a framer

    turned teacher

           by The Leader

      as punishment   and lesson

         for hurting

             his own children

   each morning

         his delicate hands

      sound

the school bell   with brute precision

     as they might

         sink a needle-

     thin nail

        with a single blow

   he lets me

     hold the bell

        its dead weight

  forged   of green-black iron

         staining my fingers

     with metallic

      ink

one afternoon

       how it begins

         I don't know

    I see Jonah's

      fear

  as he comes   through the tall

      brown grass

   light

     as a gazelle

       fast as uncle

the school watches

uncle chase him   bell held

like a club

      the big kids cheer

              as my brother

races by

    I want to say

         broken things   can be

mended

   I want to say   witness   his

blazing
speed

      I want to say   nothing

                will

            ever

    catch him

I turn away   as the bell

            completes its arc

  our parents

      pick us up early

   the oak limbs

         on the mountain road

angular as bones

     shattered then mis-set

no one believes

    the children

        and his lesson continues

I see that uncle

    years later

      pounding

  perfect squares

       in his frame shop

   I smile

     say his name

sharp as I can

   like wielding   a knife

but also

recollect

how he

wept
strange to blame him

not her

and I'm sure

there's a kinder way

to end the poem

than this:

I'm still not as big as him

Phone Call to the Pharaoh

In eighth grade Jonah leads us down the mountain
in a revolution. He calls the principal,
tells her the brainwashing is over,
that she must release the parents.
You think you are Moses?
she says, and hangs up,
the sea settling
before anyone
can cross.
Remember
racing across
the plain that opened
when you first realized
your parents couldn't save you,
towering walls of the world trembling?
Some fall in line. Some shove their way
to the far side. The poet discovers a valuable
looking sand dollar. *Focus please,* Jonah says, waves
crashing against the phone booth. *I need a real quarter.*

A Simple Equation Called Childhood

The Leader sees
the older kids are trouble
so she ends the school
and sends us out into the world.
I am in sixth grade,
and to say farewell,
our class decides to stage a play.
I'm cast as a mathematician,
ironic as I'm failing multiplication.
Miranda is my vengeful wife
who murders me.
Both dead in the last act,
we sneak to the meadow,
collapsing worlds
safer to view from afar.
I tell Miranda
kids with knives pack
public schools,
and with my math skills,
I'll wear a dunce's hat,
a practice I've witnessed
in teen movies.
Miranda sighs and says
in six years
she'll be in Harvard.
Then she grabs me,
a wild panic in her eyes,
and she blurts out
What's seven times eight!
I answer slowly,
having readied myself
for something else.
See, she says.
Nothing to worry about.

Somewhere South My Uncle Forgets Us

As a kid
nothing terrifies me more
than Dei the ram.
When he escapes,
we run for our lives.
This is no joke.
We have seen him bend
the steel gate with his nose,
and he put one uncle
in the hospital.

Uncle Tom
played football in college.
In our book,
this makes him a superhero,
a fact confirmed
by arms thick as our waists.
When Dei escapes,
Uncle Tom takes a football stance
and winks at us.
We expect their bodies
to collide,
a cloud of wool, bicep, and dust,
but at the last second,
uncle slips to one side,
deft as a dancer.

He disappears at midnight
with his family,
the first of us to flee.
No one says a word.
Over the years,
I hear rumors,

mostly about The Leader,
and a man who faced
losing everything.
No one is forcing us to stay.
People never tired
of saying this.
As if it explained anything.
I used to imagine my uncle,
somewhere far away,
missing us.

Just the other day,
his daughter Miranda
called me
and listed the steps
The Leader took
to steal my parents' life savings.
Now you see, she said,
her voice more sad than accusing.
It took thirty years
for this call
to get through to me.

Uncle Tom knew something
we didn't.
A ram can kill you,
but it also can't change course.
As Dei flew by,
uncle swept him onto his rump.
He told us that
some things are too strong
to tackle head on.
We crept forward, ready to run.

In his massive arms,
the ram lay
still as a man bound.

I Trade My Brother for Basketball

Leaving the cult
for the first time,
I feel like an alien
swinging my space boots
down from mother's
hiccupping Datsun,
my first year
down from the mountain,
public middle school
one small step for me,
one giant leap for nobody.

I start a list
of everyone I meet,
so I won't lose them,
as I lost the mountain.
I learn the lunch-room
barter economy, haggling
for gray creamed corn
and pig-pink franks.
At noon, I stalk
the basketball court
where eighth-graders glide
rim to rim, cawing
like birds for the fast break,
the long bomb,
jeans pegged so tight
they can fly.

Jonah follows me,
mountain breath hot on my neck,
his heroic size
only making it hard to hide.

Someone asks how I know him.
Who? I caw quietly,
a pair of wings
budding from my back.

After school I practice,
crossovers and elbow jumpers,
the chain-hung hoop
singing the magic pause
between catch and release,
before the ball concedes
flight to concrete.
I want to exist
in that moment.

I dream of the NBA,
where no one ever forgets
your name,
and I learn to peg my pants
to the knee,
to caw for the long pass,
the good pass,
calves wrapped tight and smooth
as airfoils.

My brother calls to me,
but I can't hear.
I am too far away already,
hoisting my body
into the sky.

Nice shooting,
a new name says.
I add it to the list,
then keep practicing,
forging precious armor
from a chain net.

If you are lost

start at the grave you dug
in the bark carpet of the eucalyptus grove

on the back acres
where hairline cracked and ton-heavy branches

told a future of certain falling
where your brothers built four walls

tongue-and-groove tight
as your single year of brotherhood

stolen cigarettes
tasting of freedom and ash

go up Crane Canyon
to the blind curve

where the dead biker gazed at you
from the pavement

through the redwood glen
for sale or sold or possibly bulldozed

to the top of the mountain
adulthood will reduce to a foothill

and nostalgia
make Olympus again

here is the pond where good and evil
both saluted you

here is the house
with a secret door the size of a child

here the bathroom
where you were punished

The Leader's perfume
forever linked to the smell of a toilet

go now to the room
where your grandmother died

cigarette bobbing on a lip
staring like a caught deer at death

heart pumping
into a shredded net of veins

proceed to the buckskin teepee
where Uncle Abe helps you string

an impossibly stiff bow
Easy for the gods, he says

pay attention as he manually expresses
a dead skunk's stink gland

dream of using this
as generals dream of nuclear weapons

cross the corporation yard
where skeins of wire weep rust

past the sandbox
where you played naked

before joining the jury
of the bluest eye

leap onto the balance beam
that proved you were brave

ignore the pecking hens
that proved you were not

listen to the scatterbrained gobble
of flesh-bearded turkeys

necks petted still
against your aunt's knife

here is the ram
bludgeoning the gate

graciously set him free
then watch him attack you

try to pet the rearing kids
who butt skulls with a dull click

but have beards soft as kittens
when they nuzzle in your palm

careful of the bristled sow portly as a cow
her injured runt bottle-fed in the tub

a squealing castaway
that you rocked like a child

and here is Dusty pulling back
fat pony lips to nip a finger

your heart leaping
when Ellen cracks her whip

the eldest girl, all hips and curly hair,
very sick then miraculously better

a mystery standing in a northern meadow
legs brown as her boots

run from the oak
that cracks like a starting gun

then nose dives into the walkway
air rushing everywhere

and you breathlessly alive
who had just been standing there

walk now under the manzanitas
bark red as a slaughtered goat's skin

think back to how your dog
licked the bloody driveway for days

stand whistling all morning
your half-blind retriever lying in a ditch

abandon the bay tree whose leaves
the big kids plug in your nose: *Now you're high*

cross the north creek
that you must not cross

but once haunted and because what you imagine
is so much more radiant than what is

go further
crawling through blackberry

leaving this world behind
to live alone forever

except here am I
reaching into the bramble's heart

thorn-scored arm extracting its fruit
stained fingers sweet as I offer it

now lie with me
in this lost meadow

beneath derelict vines
gnarled as fists

every split knuckle
punching at the sky

Return

Tell Us About Your People

At university
I study intentional communities,
which is the nice way
academics say the word cult.
When I mention mine,
the students go bonkers
and ask me everything.
Was their sex, or violence,
or at least drugs and rock-n-roll?
People, the professor says,
let's not treat him
like a subhuman.
We then discuss
the Kool-Aid cult,
and everyone
keeps an eye
on my water bottle.

Turns Out Rat Shit Is Very Unhealthy

I left home at seventeen
to see the world.
At twenty-two I had seen enough
and came home to the cult.
The student in me couldn't resist.
I'd never seen anything like it.
Also, I'm afraid to say, it was home.
The Leader put me in a barn
full of storage and rat shit
as a lesson in humility.
She was like a ghost now,
reclusive on the mountain
while all but her closest servants
lived in the valley compound.
The phone would ring
and everyone would freeze,
someone finally daring to answer.
They would nod for an hour,
then pass the phone
With each call,
everything would change:
one day we lived in tents,
the next in RVs,
then certain people
were moved out,
exiled or put in barns.
Even simple domestic chores
could serve as spiritual warfare,
toilet cleaning a fine line
between punishment and lesson.
The adults tiptoed about,
afraid The Leader
would suddenly appear

and assign them one more annoying
life-saving task.
I was an adult now,
and the chaos of my youth
was suddenly clear.
In the teachings,
one must be awake to the world
at every moment,
so she kept us in a state of shock,
always changing tactics,
until exhaustion broke us,
and we agreed
whatever she said was right,
if we could just sleep.
I watched the first generation,
nod off as The Leader spoke,
and I was jealous.
She had given them her secrets
and all I got was the aftermath.
I was also young
and loved staying up late.
Always an A student,
I took notes as The Leader
rained constructive insults
and the adults cowered.
She took me aside secretly,
said only I understood.
This was at four in the morning.
I wept to be thus chosen
and secretly gave myself an A.
The next day,
The Leader was long gone.
I walked bleary-eyed around the compound,
wanting to scream: Wake up!

My brother, also bleary-eyed, asked:
Did she wake you in the middle of the night?
Did she say only you understand?
I nodded and we walked to the barn
to shovel horse manure.
Always efficient,
she had given us both the same lie
and the same lesson.

The Shallow Subsurface of Fate

San Quentin prison faces the tide,
barred windows weeping mold.

Penned by the sea, men play basketball,
jumpsuits bright as highway flares.

A prisoner waves. It is not my brother.
A guard paces in the tower, a height

that makes the bay small as that model
we visited as children, every current

mapped, toxic spills prophesied
with hydraulic math. Fearless,

we plunged our fingers in, sent
a tsunami racing across the future

toward a house, twenty years later,
where I left my brother to drown.

Careful, the scientist said.
One slip changes everything.

Return of the Prodigal Son

The fastest runner,
and first to leave,

home from prison,
Jonah cursed us all.

Old men turned on him,
angered into youth.

You are still mine,
The Leader quietly said,

then proved herself again
by holding him

like a frightened bird
in her hands.

I followed him to the barn,
believing I could do the same.

Brother, I said.
I'm yours.

You are, he said,
then tried to break my arms.

All my life,
I've chased him,

the predator I love.
O eldest brother,

king of the recess relays,
watch me run.

A Question of War

Today   we cannot weep   because today
            we have my uncle
        who makes cabinets   in a woodshop
                half underground
        in California   where wild honey
                comes in bulk   and each night
        Orion's belt   clasps fast
                securing heaven   as we sleep.

After work   uncle Abe shows me
        his oriental swords.
                He is learning   tai-chi form,
            and the oil-dark metals
        become   in his hands   long-stemmed
                flowers   scimitar-shaped   petals
            that scythe down   with gravity
                then circle up   to stand   replanted.

I would never dream   of killing a man
        but each blade   almost
            grazes his face.   He seldom speaks of it.
                Vietnam.
            I am told   that old lie   that I
                can never   understand.
            I have seen him   as he sleeps
                kill a man.

This summer   I work in his shop.
        He teaches me to sand a corner
                until it is smooth   and soft
            and sharp   as a fresh cut.
                He teaches angles   width   and depth
        and how to craft   a box   so perfectly
                a man could sleep   inside
                            forever.

Digging With My Father

The first animal to die in my arms, she sits
three days before we bury her, death always early.

We tie dishtowels around our faces, sling her bloated
body into the wheelbarrow, take turns breathing.

She dies tied in the truck bed, strangled and trampled,
our best mother and The Leader's favorite.

I know the ties are dangerous, but say nothing.
The slick twine slips tight around her neck,

plastic and unbreakable. Her eyes bulge
as if pumped full, pupils bowling for help.

I yell at my father, pump her legs stupidly,
wonder what to tell The Leader about her goat.

The clatter of hooves grows quiet.
My father brings the wheelbarrow.

When we roll her into the grave, one leg
catches on the dull clay, running on alone.

My Dog Plays Devil's Advocate

Home from university
everyone inquired about my future.
The Leader only asked
if I'd learned to love.
She brought me the old dog
I had left behind,
half-blind with age,
that golden retriever
my first broken promise.
She had me spend night and day
beside that old friend,
gave me a red pickup
to keep until my lesson was done.
One day, moving the goats,
a kid jumped up on the cab,
its hooves playing the metal
until it hummed. I matched the note
and the truck's body resonated
like an F-150 violin.
Howling along, my dog
made a trio with man and truck.
One morning in a hurry, I left her.
She came for me but found
only darkness on the highway.
Clocks lie in September.
On a farm you dig many graves,
but I cried to lose the first being
I had named. It's not simple.
The Leader hurt people
but also, in this simple way,
tried to teach me something.
So while I'm still torn,
I know exactly
where my dog stands.

The Red Sex Wagon

Just before The Leader takes
it all, slaughters the animals,

scatters the families,
and lawsuits are all that's left,

the Red Truck takes its last ride.
Ramsey the new ram throws

his hooves up on the toolbox,
flares his nostrils above the cab.

The trees are bare, the hills dead,
and yet Ramsey smells musk

and lanolin on the autumn wind,
for it is Saturday, and we help

our father fix fences, clip hooves,
castrate lambs, and take Ramsey

up to his lady sheep. We dub it
the Red Sex Wagon

and because we are men,
we sing of fearless bandits

betrayed by their women,
and up from the lowlands

comes the Red Sex Wagon
with Ramsey, nostrils flared,

riding loose in the bed, knowing
nothing but wind and desire,

banging one cloven hoof
on the red roof of the world.

Because Brainwashing Works,
My Sister Gives Me This Poem

After my sister failed to kill herself
they put her in the chicken shed.
Naturally, she snuck out,
dyed her hair fire engine red,
then regretted it,
tried to bleach it out,
turning her head into a champagne
pink puff ball,
split and dry as yarn,
which would have been funny
except The Leader said
it was done to spite her
and had one of us
shave my sister's head
then told us all
we should fuck around,
possibly with each other,
because that's what my sister did,
my mother looking nervous,
the rest of us
avoiding eye contact,
The Leader yelling to her husband
for another martini,
all of which would be absurd,
even humorous in a movie,
and years later
I try to chuckle as my sister tells me this,
but my sister laughs too
and compares The Leader to Jabba the Hutt,
how she would wallow
in the downstairs bathtub,
slopping suds over her body

talking for hours
from an envelope of steam
much as Jabba liked to do,
who had a soft spot
for his favorites
even if he did keep them on chains,
which reminds me
I've always had a soft spot for him
with his deep stately voice
and his big belly,
the way it jostled when he laughed
as he opened that trap door
and dropped people down to their death,
people who must have known
that you can't go around disrespecting
the folks in charge,
and when I make the movie
of this lost memory
in my mind
I like the part where my pink-haired sister
yells obscenities up at Jabba
though her ankle is busted from the fall,
and I'm the one sent to wake
Jabba's pet
for today's snack.

Some Old Lady Shows Up

She comes from New Orleans
with twisted nails and a violet mole
on her chin. She smokes Marlboros
and subsists on Coke and donuts.

I ask if she is the beautiful witch
uncle Dan sings about, the one
who drowns her own children.
She's my mother, my mother says.

Todos me dicen el negro, Llorona . . .

Uncle Dan works her garden,
battling the rodents by flooding
their holes, catching a garter
by the tail who tries to escape.

The snake stretches fist-to-earth,
drowning to live. *Ay muchacho,*
my grandma says, shaking her head,
A snake will bite its own tail.

Yo soy como el chile verde, Llorona . . .

We eat pastries scented with cigarette,
and she tells of sneaking out as a girl,
riding a bumper to the bayou dance.
They could never catch me, she says.

Ambulances come, the light flooding
the garden like luminescent snakes.
She fights the EMTs who save her,
screaming for help as they help.

Y aunque me cuesta la vida, Llorona . . .

Just before she goes under, she digs
her nails into my wrist and hisses:
Ay muchacho, you are one of them.
At the hospital, I eat stale donuts.

Back home, she hides her medicine,
eats only butter, and curses the cult
for stealing her daughter. I tell her
none of this is doctor recommended.

Ay de mi Llorona, Llorona de azul celeste . . .

The Leader assigns me caretaker.
I polish my grandmother's nails,
while my uncle sings Llorona.
She no longer recognizes us.

Slipping into a coma, she grips
my arm with miraculous strength.
I pull as hard as I can but lose her.
Daylight gushes from the room.

Quien tiene amor tiene pena, Llorona . . .

My uncle still patrols her garden,
but I will always love the snakes,
those beautiful, fearful things.
Ay muchacho, nobody likes snakes.

I Thought It Was Normal Kool-Aid

The Leader sits
my grandmother in front
of us all
demanding she appreciate
what I have done for her,
living with her,
forcing her to take her pills.
I am amazed anyone dares
stand up
to that fierce old woman
who carries a knife in her purse.
Later, when I ask people
about that night
believing The Leader had finally
broken through
to my ornery old granny
and taught her to love me,
they ask if I recall
how The Leader kicked her
repeatedly
and how the doctor asked
about the bruises
and we lied.
So maybe it wasn't
enlightenment
that made my grandma weep.
Maybe it was just
the shin kicking.

A Patient Spider

In her coma, she can't even drink, so you dab a damp cue-tip to her lips to keep them from cracking. A mess of silk-thin veins extends across her face like some invisible spider slowly cocoons her. You hum the melodies of the Celtic harp record she used to play, hoping she will open her eyes, or even move her head. She claimed no past then one day started speaking Spanish to you who had traveled around the world to learn that language. She spoke French to her in-laws and also pidgin, so you try every language you know, hoping to land on the one that will wake her. When she dies, you are far away, this habit you have of leaving. You return, death so often a bridge home. Someday you will forget weeping at the funeral. You will forget your brother singing on alone, his voice strong as yours falters. You will forget that spiders still alarm you, laying their silk thread everywhere, snapping life right out of the air. Someday you will also be caught, invisible threads dragging you to the ground, and if you're lucky, some young person will hold your hand so tight it hurts. If they sing, you will recognize neither the song nor their voice, but as you drift off, you'll have a vague sense of people coming from far away, and you will want to join these kind strangers gathering at their loved one's grave.

Jazz Funeral

When my grandmother dies,
    The Leader says
   give her a Dixieland funeral,
       but New Orleans is far away
     so uncle Dan's klezmer band plays
     When the Saints
       and the local police
          stop traffic as we march
      behind the hearse, high-stepping,
   bopping umbrellas, walking
       the oldest member of our group
       into the grave,
    and I wonder if this valley
     will ever know
   that an entire people
       can begin and end here
      without a public word,
          nothing but a little traffic
    and some local nutcases
        playing wild music.

Accident on Bohemian Highway

I was already picturing a beast from the past,
when a buck dashed from the dark.

My fender spun him through the night.
Like animals, we sat, caught in our own headlights.

In the ditch, we expected antlers striking the sky,
intestines unraveling like a chord.

We found only scat, steaming on the car grill.
I have tried to wrap my sentences around

the brother I kept, and the one I lost,
but life is a dark, antlered beast,

dashing from our blind spot,
a comma, two boys shivering.

Heart's Desire

Hiking up through live oak
then down riprap steps
of abalone shell, I mimic
Uncle Abe's long stride

toward the redwood teepees
of the first people's village,
where we make arrowheads
and fire with a Wisewoman.

We twist sticks and chip obsidian
while she stories of warriors
who flew sweat lodge to creek
and now work at the mall.

I ask if I can be a Brave.
She checks my work: *Not yet*.
To this day there is nothing
I make so well as broken rock.

Hiking further, we see sandpipers
circling. My uncle knows where
they will land, but says, *Not yet,*
when I ask if he's a Wiseman.

I hike into my twenties, where
my professor calls thought a caged bird,
reminding me of my brother's parrot
smuggled here from the Amazon.

My brother didn't clip her wings,
so she headed for South America.
We found her half dead
on the beach at Heart's Desire.

I hike until my uncle is dead
and my Wisewoman gone mad,
until the footsteps I follow
on Heart's Desire are my own.

Building a Tennis Court Next to the Hospital

Uncle Will growls at his IV stand
like it's some stray dog.

He thrashes the rigging of tubes,
chuckles and says, *Half man,*

half machine, a formless robe
slack on the thin mast of his body,

his feet wide and gray against the tile.
He will never walk outside again.

It was that damn turkey, he says. Stupidly,
I wonder if cancer makes people crazy,

like my grandmother who clawed
my arm and said, *Do you see?* Water

everywhere, her mind a sinking ship.
They tell me cracklings cause cancer,

my uncle says. I am just old enough
to blame and think of the Chesterfield,

his endlessly ash-tipped sixth finger.
We stare out the window at a cold

expanse of broken earth, and I see
his other body, the one that whipped

across the court like a sail,
white cap melting into the sky.

Rain, Tell Me of an Unending Voice

I sit at our boyhood window, autumn
laying a quilt of darkness over the day,
rain breaking open my image on the glass.

In the square of light cast in the yard,
the storm-shook grass is Jonah's hair,
tussled by my father's hand. I've come
for the flotsam and jetsam of childhood.

Baby's in the cradle, brother went to town

The storm smells like my eighth birthday,
when Jonah played Moses and we followed
into the eucalyptus grove's flooded gully.

Step where I step, he yelled over the wind.
He was a good older brother, his single
rule: brother's never fight. When we met
bullies, he fought for us without a thought.

Sister's in the parlor, trying on a gown.

He came to us with a single album
at that age when each song is a dream
and in singing you can be anything.

We memorized those songs, sang them
each night, then to fiancés, at weddings,
and finally funerals, Jonah long gone.
We have forgotten they were ever his.

Mama's in the kitchen messing all around.

My father called him *Decade,* for his age,
a name I hoped to inherit. When he left,
he cried, and we sang his favorite song.

As a teenager he would not speak
to my father. Someone must have
said he was stolen. Someday I hope
we forget this also, as families must.

Papa's on the housetop and won't come down.

Decade is not lost. He still leans
into that storm, promising me my tenth
year if I can just keep up with him.

I pack my memories, leave the country.
Ten miles away, the storm passes
his house. I picture it an annoying
little brother rattling his window.

Oh the blues they come, and the blues they go.

If he looks, he'll also burst into streams,
and if rain can still be made to speak,
he will hear: Older brother, remember.

Last Passover at the Compound

We paint the doorjamb red,
safety a prayer far too often violent,

then welcome the angel anyway,
giddy for sacrifice.

The families trickle in,
like fresh rain over ruins.

Miranda's father returns,
his silent apology a leavening.

We list plagues, slay firstborns,
eat the bitter and sweet of our childhood.

Our angel crawls lap to lap,
forcing us to finger her wounds.

My father follows behind,
carrying her wings in a sack.

To me she says:
My favorite.

Miranda shrieks, *Can't you see?*
She is the pharaoh!

The angel assaults Miranda
who runs crying from the house.

You will also flee, she says,
serving me apple cobbler

as I sponge up
my best friend's blood.

In the Cult

everyone says they love you
no one leaves
everyone fears a midnight call
night is always a train wreck or a party
you never felt so alive
somewhere a phone rings
nobody answers
everyone is whispering
someone is weeping
just keep dancing
someone hands you a note
everyone is watching
one of us is not here

Exile

Electing Exile

Hung over from reminiscing,
Morphine still pumping
through the stereo,
we head to The Terrible Café.
The eggs run,
fly-shit speckles the walls,
and the waitress
wants to poison us
for making her work.
Who would ever come back here?
she growls,
flicking her order pad out
like a switchblade.
She is famous for this,
and my brother loves it,
slurping his raw egg
like a sacramental soup.
He's come home,
odd-jobbing for the aunts and uncles,
even for The Leader.
He asks about the other side of the world.
No terrible cafés, I say,
choking down
a half-frozen piece of toast,
doughy knots
of envy
expanding in my gut.

In Another Life

Quiet comes to the village market
well after dark, the streets wet

from women washing their stalls,
tomorrow covered with tarps,

and ties, and string. In that windless
tinkling of things, your heels

scrape the pavement like a horse,
this the memory I've come for.

Arirang, arirang, arario . . .

In the harbor, strange moans
sound from the docked boats.

like men on the edge of death,
or women giving birth.

In moonlight, the seawall stones
take on strange forms,

one a bird, one a man, one
a girl, playing with her hair.

Out on the horizon squid men
seduce their catch with light bulbs

so bright they look like flashlights,
hunting a lost child.

Arirang, arirang, arario . . .

A family of women divers surface,
whistle, and plunge for abalone, bird

calling for safety, fingers iron hooks,
floating baskets slowly filling with shell.

For half a century, the tide has piled
skipping stones inside the caves of war,

as if the cliffs are a god-child's playroom,
and genocide was just a bad dream.

A short throw offshore,
a sea stack marks a lover's suicide.

Some say it is just a story.
Some say stories keep us alive.

Arirang, arirang, arario . . .

Night falls on drummers dressed
in white, silk streamers on hinged

poles fixed to their heads. Rising
on the tip of their slippers,

their bows make arcs of color,
beauty wielded like a rainbow whip.

Your parents will die here,
but you're not coming home.

Arirang, arirang, arario . . .

Dawn downtown is synth music
and fluorescents and searing pork

and pepper soup and dumpling
steam hot and thick as sweat.

Silk-clad pleasure women
shuffle down alleys in pairs,

dangerous as mermaids,
bodies not on sale but a living

just the same. They come and go
talking of nothing and soju

until blue-suited businessmen
collapse in the gutters and weep.

Arirang, arirang, arario . . .

The mountain roads are basalt
walled, stacked by tangerine

men who machete the vines come
to reclaim the ancestor's grave,

where whisker-short, scissor-cut grass,
is circled by interlocking evergreens

filled with black, hook-nosed birds,
squawking as if to call death back.

Arirang, arirang, arario . . .

Dawn comes to my master's house,
his fingers tipped in hand-ground ink,

walls papered in brush strokes,
cups stained with the tea of emperors.

I have come looking for truth,
my first master mad, the second

dead, and this one promising
a new name if I agree to return.

Some say you can never go back.
Some say life is a circle.

A wood clapper starts the ceremony,
a simple will to serve, passed body to body

through war, across famine, to a song
everyone knows, but no one can explain.

Arirang, arirang, arario . . .

Exile's Kitchen: Breaking Things

I once marveled at my ability
to catch things:

wine glasses, knives, hearts.
I recall a day when it rained dishes.

I snatched each from the air,
and dried it, my hands

machines of indifference,
leaping out of their own accord.

I now marvel at their clumsiness,
making up for all those years

of obeisance. I can barely
pour a drink without killing someone.

Today, cursing my brutal hands,
worried the downstairs neighbor

will hear me destroying my life,
I marvel at the circumference

of shattered things. I sweep
high and low, in rooms

unused for years, closets
I didn't know existed.

Everywhere invisible slivers
take root, a well-groomed lawn

of invisible blades. To think
I once walked barefoot.

Tired of cutting myself,
I buy steel-soled boots,

eye every new lover
like a candy-covered razor,

clean so deeply I am sure
nothing will ever break again.

Seven Steps to the Podium
for My Uncle's Funeral

The teachings ask you, at every moment,
I am writing this in a Kristiansand hotel.
to be conscious of self, other, and world,
I left; other people cried; the world is round.
Seven steps separate heaven and hell.
Today's tiny hell is the rage of a missed bus.
Thoughtlessness is to fall down the steps.
Not the bus, the steps inside you.
Enlightenment is to walk back up the stairs.
A bit like a stair machine it seems.
It's not what you do; it's how you do it.
Unfortunately, this is also a hash tag.
Call it intention over action.
I'm drunk on the couch but have a saint's posture.
A person can save you to own you.
Or write their life just to sell it?
Life and death are a single step.
It is the age of funerals, and so we return.
Enlightenment can also be to let go.
We pick the good stories and reminisce.
But you will never stop falling.
My brothers are here, avoiding each other.
Anger is an incredible fountain of energy.
The Leader steps up to claim the dead.
He is ours, we yell, falling all over ourselves.

Continuous Return

The Prince Who Chose Hell

As children
we read the Mahabharata
dreamed of stringing
Arjuna's bow,
a weapon no mortal hand
could bend,
but the great archer dies,
and of his brothers
Yudhisthira alone
summits the sacred mountain,
a weak boy,
his only power love.
Asked if he wishes to pass
into heaven,
he chooses to follow his brothers
to hell,
tumbling down the mountain.

Who will be so brave?
The Leader asks.

When I tumble
home,
my arms raw
with the world's archery,
The Leader asks:
Still my Yudhisthira?
I face my first god
and nod,
whisper the names
we have lost,
and string
her impossible bow
with my heart.

Losing at Sorry

Sorry was a board game,
the goal to send
other players home
as you ran off to victory
somewhere not home.
We would gleefully howl
the name of the game
as we sent our competitors packing,
homecoming
the same as losing.
I was playing Sorry
when my sister was born.
Everyone was in the birth room.
The Leader said this was essential
to understand life.
I had been there but then saw
a spot of blood
on the clean sheet
near my mother's head.
I panicked.
A good poem is enough
to tear me up,
so you can guess what happened
when I thought
my mother might die.
Years later,
leaning against a car in Louisiana,
I was reminiscing
with my sister about the cult
I loved
and she had to escape
when she said:
I thought you would protect me.

Guilt and anger
fought to rule my face.
I tried to recall
her ever needing my protection.
I remember
walking past her in the hall,
her hair recently dyed,
me saying cool,
her not really smiling.
I cleared my throat,
scanned the parked cars
for someone to protect her from.
Here's what I'm saying:
nothing is perfect,
even Akhenaten's bust
can act as cover
for bloodshed,
at least this is what I told myself
when they sent my sister away,
and I spent afternoons
wondering if calling her
might interrupt
some terrifying decision
she was about to make.
The truth is,
looking at Akhenaten in Boston,
I didn't think of betrayal
or The Leader's stained divinity
but of a frightened boy
who doesn't believe he can die
and a droplet on white cotton
at my sister's birth.

I wonder if any of us change,
for I have seen the world,
even made a baby of my own,
but as I try to say the word,
to really say it,
I am the one sent home
to a dimly lit hall,
where I walk past a girl of seventeen
who is sinking
and reaches out to me,
and all I have is this flimsy poem
to offer as a raft,
this rather distracted bunch of words
about pharaohs and linens
all mumbled a bit incoherently
and out of order
as my sister stands here
in a parking lot in Louisiana
wondering why on earth I am talking
about her birth
and a board game
where you joyously yell:
Sorry.

My Mother Chooses Not to Teach

When I ask my mother
for the teachings

she starts in her kitchen
that smells of seared onion

and last night's wine,
then leads me out the window

to a century old oak standing
on a path cut in conquest,

over a mountain
older than human time,

ground up from a planet
ancient as a light particle,

circling a star where if you sat
with a smoke you could spot

Centauri's triple sun
just a smidge past Pluto,

the galaxy a creek
at your feet.

Now turn around,
look down here,

aim your fall
like a time machine

or a meteor, past moons
and Big Bang tidbits,

toward this town, this room,
your mother's footprint.

Too slow to follow,
I chase her thoughts

like a lone bird
trying to cross a century,

migrating dawn to dawn
to reach this morning

where an insignificant mote of dust
is now half star, half home

as it circles my mother's hand,
which now opens to reveal my own,

as she snuffs the candle and decides
she cannot say all she knows

of distant planets
and the child's heart.

The Last Followers

My parents spent
thirty years in her house,
raising her children
washing her dishes,
then she kicked them out
without a penny,
like old servants
in some grand English manor.
The Leader
actually was English
and thought of herself as a queen,
so maybe it's all
a cultural misunderstanding.
But this is America,
and we are quite thick-headed.
Thus it was that my parents told her
to go fuck herself,
using the correct legal terms,
of course.
It took a decade,
my father grew sick,
and we lost everything,
but my parents did finally force
the queen to nod,
slightly,
which is immense
if you believe in queens.

After All Is Said and Done

All I can say is this:
It ends in a parking lot,

a millennium later,
the animals butchered,

lands mortgaged,
my parents in exile.

All communities implode,
my sociologist friend says.

It's quite fascinating.
I try to avoid sociologists.

We stop as The Leader
approaches, her hands

trembling with hope
or sickness, or just rage.

Only you returned to me,
she says, then stumbles.

She is crippled now.
We help her to her car.

Then we buy bread and milk.
She's a dangerous, brilliant woman

who won't apologize.
I can only say, Goodbye.

For The Leader

I have thought many times
of visiting you,
to do the dishes
or help you up the stairs,
for though my pity
will anger you,
I often feel
you were also wounded,
and because you were kind to me
I feel it my duty
to return,
as I did so many years ago,
but what I fear most
is this:
though I have spent
my life studying
you will turn on me,
call me stupid.
Then,
as if to prove your point,
I'll say,
I still love you.

Map of Continuous Return

My mother sows the past
into her garden. It sprouts

names I have not spoken
in years. Her grandchild

plucks them as if she fears
nothing. *Was this your childhood?*

she asks. *It tastes so sweet
it hurts.* I stomp about,

carving my name on stones.
Put those back, my mother says.

Geese circle, our field marked
in the avian collective mind.

My daughter shades her eyes,
as white forms descend,

legs dropping like dowsing
sticks for water. *Migration*

is not leaving, my mother says.
It's a map of continuous return.

My daughter takes my hand
and asks why they fly in a V.

I think of the strength
it takes to break open the sky.

Some are brave, I say.
Others are meant to follow.

She looks at my mother:
You said they take turns.

A Child's Christmas on the Mountain

for the Groupers

Every year the uncles build a Christmas village on the mountain, a maze of storefronts and straw-covered stages that rises like buzz-saw magic from the upper meadow. Christmas morning hundreds arrive, loaded with beef stew, cider and pies. In the afternoon, Santa comes in a carriage, the driver a stranger who scowls when we call him uncle. The older kids interrogate him slyly about the outside world while he stands like a phantom in the twilight fog, hands stabbed into his overcoat, leaning a little toward his horses, who sweat and clop their hooves nervously, already tasting their evening oats.

After two days of school plays and the subtle propaganda of Santa reading our peccadillos from a colossal tome, it grows late and the young adults sneak off in pairs to the pond. If we stay late enough, we get to watch the aunties drink too much and bawl and ferociously hug us, saying, *You'll never know how wonderful this is.* Then we curl up by the rusted oil barrels that are filled with logs and set alight, resting our shoes against the metal until they melt.

The year trouble begins, the adults are sealed in the main house and The Leader's anger is like bad weather settling over everything, the thunder of her voice echoing across the plywood village. She talks for ten hours straight, one family is exiled, and we are not allowed to eat. Adults rush to and fro but tell us nothing. I follow the big kids into the woods, and they help me up to the platform at the top of the giant oak. They agree it's all mind control and soon we'll escape and not have to live together. Someone pulls out a smoke and hands it around, and because everyone laughs when I reach for it, I lean bravely over the platform edge, the vertigo so abrupt, Jonah has to pull me back before I fall.

Out in the world, they are dropping bombs and inventing vaccines and other things of which we are ignorant and yet certain we will outdo. In the distance, the Christmas village looks like an old movie, frames flickering into existence by the light of the bonfires.

Then our names are called, and though someone makes a heroic claim to never go home, everyone agrees it's too cold for revolution, and we scramble down the trunk, Miranda sprinting first across the meadow, the front bird in a jagged line of shadows drifting back to the only thing we have ever known.

A Note on the Text

This work was born out of a childhood spent in one of the longest running intentional communities in the United States. Based on the teachings of G.I. Gurdjieff and run by one of his second-generation students, "The Group" never had an official name and has neither been studied nor written about officially.

Over a period of forty years, this group married, had children, started daycares, a school, and multiple businesses, experimented in communal living, worked on communal projects, and on occasion participated in the radical and questionable practice of child sharing. All this was haunted by cult accusations against The Leader.

For many years I saw the community through rose-colored glasses. I wrote a BA thesis called *Utopian Dreams* and returned with my brother to teach the next generation. Friends thought I was brainwashed. The Leader went from the genius of the group to a solitary and vengeful recluse. Eventually, like everyone in my generation, I left.

There has never been an official name for the group. As children, we hid the fact that we had hundreds of aunts and uncles. We wanted to be like everyone else. "The Group" became a term of convenience, and we referred to ourselves as "groupers." I live across the globe now, but I visit as often as I can. I continue to deeply love my aunts and uncles.

This is a creative work, so I have occasionally combined people to clarify narrative. All names have been changed. I promise. It's not you.

Acknowledgments

Grateful acknowledgment is made to the editors and readers at these publications, in which the following poems have appeared, often in earlier versions:

American Journal of Nursing: "Building a Tennis Court Next to the Hospital"

Cobalt Review: "Digging With My Father," "Tips on Student Engagement"

Georgia State University Review: "A Student of Celestial Things"

Korea Lit: "In Another Life"

Pa'lante!: "Children of Utopia"

Plume: "Exiles Kitchen: Breaking Things"

Ponder Review: "A Tiny Solar System Called the Heart"

Slipstream: "A Map of Continuous Return"

The Southern Poetry Anthology: Louisiana: "I Will Make You Fishermen"

Third Wednesday: "Jazz Funeral," "Rain Tell Me of an Unending Voice," "My Dog Plays Devil's Advocate"

Timber: "Why I Am a Writer"

Two Hawks Quarterly: "A Question of War"

Under the Gum Tree: "If You Are Lost"

Whale Road Review: "First Loss"

My gratitude to Karen Kelsay and everyone at Kelsay Books. Special thanks to all my teachers over the years, particularly Lisa Chavez, Joy Harjo, Skip Fox, Martha Reed, and the adjunct who taught me the translation course at UCSC, the woman I credit for awakening the poet in me. I'm sorry I've lost your name. To the poet Luis Garcia Montero, with whom I studied Lorca's work in Granada, a city I blame for turning me into a serious poet. Thanks to early readers, most notably John Sibley Williams, whose comments were essential, and also Elizabeth J. Colen. I also want to acknowledge the "Groupers" I grew up with and who cared for me in so many ways. Thank you to Alejandro Escudé, who used to carry his clothes in a guitar case. One day in our college dorm, he taught me to stop hiding this habit called poetry. To Andy Merriss, friend, brother, and fellow artist, who I was supposed to thank in my first book. To my family. The best. I miss you. And, as always, to Adria. Marry me?

About the Author

Allen C. Jones has an MFA in poetry from the University of New Mexico and a PhD in English from the University of Louisiana at Lafayette. He serves as associate professor of literature and culture at the University of Stavanger in Norway. His research concerns the pedagogical use of Surrealist literary games and the creative potential of experimental composition. His debut novel *Her Death Was Also Water* came out from Midnight Sun Publishing in 2022, and a short story collection is forthcoming. His poetry and fiction appear widely.

Find links to his publications, digital games, and research: allencjones.com.

Follow him on social media: allencjones_theauthor